The Three-R

PASSAU

„The Venice of Bavaria"

An Illustrated Guide to the Historical Old Town and its Districts

A historical view of Kloster-Mariahilf (Our Lady of Succour Monastery), taken from the bank of the Inn near the Schaiblingsturm.

Text: Wolfgang Kootz
Photographs: Willi Sauer, Ulrich Strauch

Verlag & Design Simon Sauer

Welcome to Passau, the City of the Nibelungs!

The Nibelungenlied, the most famous epic poem in the German language, tells of Kriemhild's arrival in „Pazzovwe", passed this way during the migration of peoples, as did the armies of Emperor Frederick I on their crusades, the trad-

Passau, the "floating city", with the Innstadt district (far left), the old town

where she is received by her uncle, Bishop Pilgrim. Thus centuries ago, the city at the junction of the Danube, Inn, and Ilz rivers was already a centre of trade and travel between East and West, North and South. The settlers ers coming from the Mediterranean and the salt deposits in the foothills of the Alps, and, last but not least, the Bavarian princess Elisabeth, popularly known as „Sissi", on her way to the Imperial Throne of Austria. The city got its name from one of the Roman forts in the vicinity: „Batavis" was corrupted into „Passawe", which ultimately became „Passau". Among those who profited from the city's favourable position were the prince bishops, whose sphere the wealth of the merchants are reflected even today in the magnificent buildings, such as St. Stephen's Cathedral, the Town Hall assembly rooms, the defiant citadel Veste Oberhaus, and the residence of the sovereigns.

around the cathedral, and the Ilzstadt at the foot of Veste Oberhaus.

of influence extended eastward all the way into parts of what is now Hungary. They ruled over a bishopric which, in terms of geographical area, was once the largest in the entire Holy Roman Empire of the German Nation. Their power and Under their influence, Passau also developed into an educational and cultural centre that lives on today in the city of schools and universities and its varied cultural landscape. Besides renowned museums and galleries,

3

theatre, operas, and concerts of all kinds make for a varied arts calendar, rounded out by an attractive cabaret and the „European Weeks", a music festival which receives a great deal of international attention and is dedicated to the ideal of European unity. In addition to the weekly evening concerts in the cathedral, in summer, visitors can enjoy a daily thirty-minute noon-time concert on the world's largest church organ. Artisans and craftspeople are concentrated mainly in Höllgasse whilst the large public spring and autumn festivals "Maidult" and Herbstdult" take place at Kohlbruck Exhibition Park with its new Three Nations Hall. In Passau, however, hospitality is second nature all year round. Whether in the numerous, earthy beer gardens and taverns or the sidewalk cafés of the extensive pedestrian precinct, visitors will quickly find a place where they feel at home. Just shopping the numerous boutiques, shops, and department stores or the atmospheric weekly market is a pleasure every bit as unforgettable as sauntering through the romantic alleyways and the dreamy corners of the old town and along its riverfront promenades. Even night-owls will find plenty of opportunities to indulge their proclivities in Passau.

If it's outdoor exercise you're looking for, you'll find it in Passau. The city has an exemplary network of hiking trails, offers many possibilities for water sports, and is a hot tip among cyclists, with no fewer than eight long-distance cycling routes leading in all directions. There is even a day-or-night repair service and a plain hotel geared to ecology-minded cyclists. Guest houses and hotels steeped in tradition court the favour of Passau's visitors with hospitality and tasteful furnishings. These visitors now also include many conference participants, since more and more hotels have begun offering space suitable for such occasions. The Passau Fleet's riverboats are also chartered time and again for such events. Even „normal" visitors, however, shouldn't miss the experience of a boat trip on the Danube, for there is scarcely another place on earth where they will have such a large selection. Whether up the Danube to Deggendorf or downstream to Engelhartszell, Schlögener Schlinge, Linz, Vienna, Budapest, or even further, whether for Sunday brunch or evenings with dancing or jazz, or even just the forty-five minute tour of the three rivers: A boat trip is a treat not to be missed when in Passau. Of course, this city near the Austrian and Czech borders is also a suitable starting point for outings to the Bavarian Forest, Munich, Vienna, Budapest, Prague, or Salzburg. Note however that, as in many old cities, parking is crowded at best. For this reason, there are only toll parking lots in downtown Passau, most of which close evenings or nights. Thus it is advisable to use the Park & Ride facilities or the parking lot at Veste Oberhaus (15 minutes by foot, shuttle bus available). The transit authority offers discount day tickets for guests, making it easier for even the most passionate motorist to leave the driving to someone else for a change.

The following pages cover the sights of Passau in more detail, describing a tour of the old town as well as outings to the city's other districts. Those who are interested in historic Passau's vast historical legacy will quickly realise that even a thorough visit of the one-time residence of the prince bishops is no one-day affair. So we wish you plenty of time to enjoy your stay. Above all, we hope you take pleasure in using this guide.

The history of the City of Passau

5000	BC Earliest evidence of human habitation in the Passau region.
5000	BC Human settlement in the area of the present-day city.
5th - 1st century BC	Major fortified settlement of the Celts in the area of the modern-day Old Town. Brisk trade in graphite and salt.
1st - 5th century AD	Roman forts in what later became the old town (Batavis) and the Innstadt (Biotro) guard both the northern border of the Roman Empire along the Danube and the border between the provinces of Raetien in the west and Norikum (east of the Inn). The modern city name „Passau" is derived from the Latin „Batavis".
5th cent. AD	Saint Severinus, the patron saint of Bavaria and Austria, founds a little monastery near the present-day Church of St. Severinus in what is now the Innstadt district.
739	By order of the Pope, Bonifatius confirms Passau's status as an episcopal see.
Ca. 740	Niedernburg Abbey founded. Endowed with vast tracts of land, the abbey is granted immediacy in 1010.
789	Emperor Charlemagne decrees that Passau's rival city, Salzburg, shall be the archiepiscopal see.
977	One of Emperor Otto II's armies lays siege to Passau, taking the city by storm.
9th century	St. Stephen's Cathedral in Passau is named the „Mother Church of the Roman Catholic Eastern Danube".
999	The bishops of Passau are accorded lordship over the city and (1611) the lands of Niedernburg Abbey.
1100	There is a castle in the modern-day district of Hals.
1133	A wooden bridge over the Inn replaces the ferry.
1164	First mention of the „Herbstdult" as a trade fair.
1209	A defensive wall also encloses the Neustadt district.
1217	Emperor Frederick II invests Bishop Ulrich with the title of prince bishop, thus dashing the hopes of Passau's citizens that their city would be granted the status of a free imperial town.
1219	Construction begins on the „Oberhaus", the defiant citadel of the prince bishops.
1257	The „Ilzstadt" is mentioned in documents as the point of departure of the „Golden Path", which is important for trading in salt with Bohemia.
1278	Passau's second bridge now spans the Danube.
1367	Renewed uprising of Passau's citizenry against the rule of the prince bishops. The rebellion is put down once and for all at the bloody Battle of Erlau.
1407	Cornerstone of the late Gothic cathedral laid.
1408	Completion of the defensive walls around the Innstadt and Ilzstadt districts.
1476	Pogrom: Numerous Jews are murdered following a supposed „sacrilege against the host"; their synagogue is razed. The Salvatorkirche (St. Salvator's Church) is built in its place, as „atonement".
1501	During the „Great Flood", the high-water mark reaches 11.5 m, surpassing all high-water marks recorded since 1173 and down to the present day. The Danube and the Inn join before even reaching the old town.

1552	The Treaty of Passau between Emperor Charles V and Elector Moritz of Saxony is the precursor of the Peace of Augsburg (1555).
1568	Bavaria founds its own salt works on the Inn, which has a disastrous effect on Passau.
1624-27	Construction of the present-day pilgrimage church of Mariahilf (Our Lady of Succour).
1634	The plague rages in Passau, and again in 1650.
1662	The Great Fire devours the entire old town.
1668	Construction starts on the present-day Baroque cathedral
1676	Imperial wedding: Leopold I marries in Passau.
1683	Emperor Leopold resides in Passau during the Turks' siege of Vienna.

1712-30	Construction of the new residence.
1789	First porcelain-making operation in Passau, trade in china clay.
1803	The Bishopric of Passau is annexed to Bavaria.
1805	The French Emperor Napoleon I visits Passau, and again in 1809.
1806	Niedernburg Abbey closed.
1862	Empress Elisabeth of Austria, popularly known as „Sissi", visits Passau.
1867	Citadel Veste Oberhaus decommissioned.
1910	Suspension bridge erected over the Danube.
1953	Cultural festival „European Weeks" founded.
1954	Record flooding with a high-water mark well over 10 m, even higher than in 1899. Afterward, 18-year reconstruction of the riverside thoroughfare „Uferstraße" in the Ilz district, for which an entire row of houses is demolished.
1979-80	Refurbishing and expansion, in St. Stephen's Cathedral, of the world's largest church organ.
2004	The building of „Hall of the Three Nations" with exhibition centre in Kohlbruck
2008	Neue Mitte. New Shopping Center

7

Auf fröhlicher Welle

Boat Trips from Passau

Three river trip
Every day, regularly March-beginning November and 26th-31st December

Passau-Linz-Passau
Daily 9 am except Mondays (28/04-08/10)

Passau-Engelhartszell-Schlögen and back
Daily 12 am Passau, 1.30 pm Engelhartszell, 2.10 pm Schlögen/2.25 pm Schlögen, 3.25 pm Engelhartszell, 5.15 pm Passau (23.04. - 09.10.) + daily except Mondays 9 am Passau, 2.05 pm Linz/2.20 pm Linz, 8.40 pm Passau (29/04-09/10) with stop at Engelhartszell (going 10.30 am, back 6.45 pm) and Schlögen (going 11.05 am and back 5.55 pm)

Spare ribs and music
Every Friday at 7.30 pm (July-September)

Music and Dancing
Every Saturday at 7 pm (30/04-22/10)

Trip with buffet on board of the gala boat "Regina Danubia"
Every Sunday at 12 am (24/04-23/10)

Trips with special subjects
For ex. the Danube "on fire"

Passau-Wachau-Vienna (2 days)
Departure every Friday

Fine food and drinks available on all excursion boats
Discounts for children, families and groups
Ask for our complete timetable

Donauschiffahrt
WURM + KÖCK

Donauschiffahrt Wurm + Köck · Höllgasse 26 · D-94032 Passau
Phone 08 51/92 92 92 · Fax: 3 55 18 · e-mail: info@donauschiffahrt.de
www.donauschiffahrt.de

A tour of the old town

At the town hall

Our tour of the old town begins and ends at the square in front of the town hall, Rathausplatz, which was once the fish market. Located on the banks of the Danube, it can also be reached by way of the suspension bridge from the Ilzstadt district. The excursion boats head out from here for the obligatory threerivers tour, as does the shuttle bus to Veste Oberhaus. Guests can get suggestions at the nearby **Tourist-Information Office** ❶. It is on the Danube-side of the Neue Rathaus (new town hall), a one-time brewery building that forms the west flank of Rathausplatz. The square is dominated by the slender, neo-Gothic (1889-92)

Rathausturm („town hall tower"), the legitimate successor of a building with a defensive tower which the citizenry acquired as a **Rathaus (town hall)** ❷ at the then fish market in 1322. According to the inscription on the Schrottgasse side, the tower is already mentioned as the town hall in official records from 1298. The citizenry, however, soon had to return it, together with the town bell and the town seal, to the possession of the prince bishop. After much squabbling, the citizens were finally able to take uncontested possession of the building in 1396. The high-water marks from past centuries on the Rathausplatz side bear witness to the citizens' constant struggle against the forces of nature, which, during 1954's record

The town hall tower with the old and, at far right, the new town hall; between them, the highly traditional hotel „Wilder Man". The spires and the East Choir of the Cathedral of St. Stephen are seen above the new town hall.

A view of the old town with the towers of the town hall and the Jesuit Church. The Mariahilf-Kloster (Our Lady of Succour Monastery) is seen in the background.

flood, nearly reached the high-water mark of the Great Flood of 1501. The city had the present-day carillon (which, incidentally, is the largest in Bavaria) installed in the tower in 1991. To the east - connected by a round-arched loggia - it is adjoined by the magnificently painted Saalbau or „hall building", which was erected around 1400 on the site of two houses which were purchased and demolished. Altogether, the old town hall alone consists of eight buildings that were joined to form a whole in the late 19th century. At that time, the old portal in the centre of the hall building façade was converted into a window. A little further to the left, another portal leads into the rathskeller, which the city established in 1895. While the paint-

The town hall *assembly rooms can be viewed: April – Oct. and Saturday before 1st. Advent, 6th Jan. 10:00 AM - 4:00 PM (except during special events),*
Town hall carillon: *daily at 10:30 AM / 2:00 / 3:30 / 5:30 PM.*

ings by F. Wagner were largely destroyed by the 1954 flood, Walter Mauder created an interesting picture of the „Passau Blockhead" before the backdrop of the Great Fire of 1662. As tradition would have it, the head, which was found later, once belonged to a monumental figure of the Gothic cathedral and fell to the ground back then. After first turning up at a canon's court in the street known as „Steinweg", it landed (having made several other stops along the way) at Veste Oberhaus, where it still sits in hiding despite much negotiating and conferring. A 1904 plaque commemorates Empress Elisabeth of Austria, the daughter of the Bavarian Baron Max, for whom Passau was the last stop on her bridal journey to Vienna. In 1862, she even came for a six-day family reunion, during which time she stayed at the Hotel „Wilder Mann" adjacent to the Rathaus.

The present-day town hall portal is in Schrottgasse. A late Gothic (ca. 1500) sculpture is preserved above the lintel: it shows the figure of a girl with Passau's mascot, the wolf, flanked by two men. Inside, on the way to the two town hall assembly rooms, painstakingly built models of medieval ships are exhibited in a display case. The creator of one of the authentic cogs, which are made of amber, spent up to 3500 hours working on it.

The Great Fire of 1662 didn't spare the town hall either, but repair work began that same year. The vaulted ceilings with the elaborate stucco work (created by Giovanni Battista Carlone, who also did the stucco work in the cathedral) and the two portals with their door leafs all date from this time. The huge painting, however, was created by the historical painter Ferdinand Wagner, one of Passau's most famous inhabitants. While the painting was only created starting in 1886, it is a perfect replica of Baroque style. The Großer Rathaussaal („Great Assembly Room"), which is still used

The Great Assembly Room in the Town Hall: Kriemhild's arrival in Passau (Painting by F. Wagner).

The imposing Great Assembly Room in Town Hall, designed by Carlo Lurago

12

(architecture), Battista Carlone (stucco work), and Ferdinand Wagner (paintings).

for cultural events today, shows scenes from the history of the city, including the Nibelungenlied. One painting shows Kriemhild's arrival in Passau at the side of her uncle, Bishop Pilgrim. (The artist immortalised himself here in the form of a blond groom). In another, the Danube

Leopold I was wedded to Eleonore of Palatinate-Neuburg by Prince Bishop Sebastian von Pötting. Many additional scenes are furnished with years in Roman numerals and allegories. The tastefully adapted, elaborate glass windows (1891) also present Passau motifs. The West

water-nymphs warn Hagen. Another colossal painting shows the Imperial Wedding of 1676, when Emperor

Window is crowned by the coat-of-arms of the Bavarian reigning dynasty and the Passau coat-of-arms, the red wolf on a

Ceiling painting in the Small Assembly Room at Town Hall: the three rivers at the feet of Passavia.

<-- *The walls and ceilings of the Small Assembly Room in Town Hall are also magnificently decorated.*

white background. The presentation of the coat-of-arms by Bishop Wolfker is depicted on the ceiling of the Kleiner Rathaussaal („Lesser Assembly Room"), as is the homage of the three rivers, Inn (a wild muscleman with an uprooted tree), Danube, and Ilz to „Passavia" before the backdrop of Passau's old town. Because it is often in use, especially for weddings and meetings, the Lesser Assembly Room is not always open for viewing.

Before we leave the Rathaus, let us cast a glance at the northern inner court. The free-standing fountain is decorated by the granite figure of the „Passauer Lindl", a contemporary sculpture in the historical style of a Roland. Near the present-day portal is a plain wooden door painted with a hat and the inscription „He who finds authority a thing to scoff, not dread, / Needn't be surprised to find this hat upon

his head". This was once the entrance to the gaol „Zum Roten Hut" („At the Sign of the Red Hat"). Starting in 1546, this gaol, together with the women's gaol „Zur Hörndlin" and the madhouse, was housed in the town hall. At the West Portal of the Rathaus, we turn to face the fish market again. The Danube side of the square, which is open today, was once closed by a wall, two gates, and a tower. A cookshop, two fountains, and a permanent building with the fish sellers' stands made for very cramped quarters. On the east, where the main customs office stands today, the square bordered on the municipal dance hall. In 1528, the hall served as a venue for celebrations, dancing, and theatrical performances; an attached tavern was for smaller meetings with wine and beer. The Royal Customs Office took up quarters here in 1806.

15

The landing stage for cruise ships.

A walk around the point

The Fritz-Schäffer-Promenade leads us between the main customs office and the Danube to Römerplatz („Romans' Square") at the southern bridgehead of the Prince Regent Luitpold Bridge, which is known simply as „the suspension bridge" in Passau. Completed in 1910, it replaced Germany's oldest pedestrian bridge, called the Kettensteg or „Chain Bridge", which had spanned the 115 meter wide Danube since 1869. Ferdinand Wagner, the historical painter and honorary citizen of Passau, was vehemently opposed to construction of the new bridge and felt this was a gross disfigurement of Passau's scenic beauty. When his protests were ignored, he sold his home, the castle Veste Niederhaus, moved to Munich, and never returned to his home town again. Even today, however, the bridge still hangs from its two 25-cm thick steel suspension cables. It is functional perhaps, but not much to look at, although watched over by St. John of Nepomuk, the patron saint of bridges. The street called Bräugasse begins diagonally opposite. Part of the present-day university dormitory on the left side occupies the „Kettensteggebäude" („chain bridge building"). This building was used as a salt shed until 1829, then served (1869-1910) as the gatehouse of

Busy shipping at the suspension bridge below the fortress Veste Oberhaus.

Museum Moderner Kunst (Museum of Modern Art):
all year around Tuesday - Sunday 10 am - 6 pm, except 1. Nov. - 6. Jan.
11 am - 5 pm, Phone (0851) 383879-0, Fax 383879-79
www.mmk-passau.de, E-Mail: info@mmk-passau.de

Gothic architecture and modern art.

Museum of Modern Art: Fascinating contrasts in old rooms.

the aforementioned chain bridge. The adjoining building, a historic old town edifice, houses the Wörlen Foundation's **Museum of Modern Art ❸**. Here one can view 20th century artwork in changing exhibitions. A memorial plaque commemorates the Church of St. Marien, the church of Niedernburg Abbey (from the 8th cent.) which stood on this site from 1130 until it fell victim to the Great Fire of 1662. On this side, a gateway to the spacious abbey grounds and three painted round arches survive. Turning left into the street called Hirschwirtsgasse, we come to the Danube quay with additional landing places for riverboats with regularly scheduled and cruise service. Already in Roman times under Emperor Justinian,

19

the Danube was an important route that led, whether by boat or along the banks, to Eastern Europe. According to legend, it was used by the Nibelungs. In this most famous German epic, Kriemhild visits her uncle Pilgrim, who was Bishop of Passau 971-991 (the scene is portrayed in the Great Assembly Room at Town Hall). Frederick I Barabarossa also used the river on his crusade to the Holy Land, and Passau opened the door to trade with the East. This was joined by the Inn as a connection to the salt deposits in Salzburg and Bavaria including trade all the way to Venice and the entire Mediterranean. So it comes at no surprise that, in the Middle Ages, more goods were transferred in Passau alone than in the famous Middle Rhine.

It was only after the discovery of America that the trade routes shifted northward and to the seaports.

Today, the historic route along the Bavarian and Austrian Danube is used primarily by tourists travelling with Germany's largest Danube fleet (Wurm & Köch) to Deggendorf in Bavaria or - past castles and palaces - to Engelhartszell or by way of Schlögener Schleife to Linz. The big cruisers even sail as far as Eastern Europe. Visitors to Passau should make sure to at least take the three-rivers tour, for it offers incomparable views of the „floating town" and its looming, chimney-like towers. The accompanying narration offers a preliminary overview of Passau's history and sights. Especially when seen from the Inn, the riverside promenade calls Italy to mind, which is another reason why Passau is known as the „Venice of Bavaria". One reason for this was flourishing trade with Italy, which also brought Italian cultural influences, including craftsmen and artists, to the Danube; another reason was the fire prevention ordinance enacted in the wake of the Great Fire of 1662, which prescribed walls extending beyond the eaves. Here at **Dreiflüsse-Eck („Three-Rivers Corner")** ❹, there is a lovely view of the mouth of the Ilz and the fortresses Niederhaus and Oberhaus with the interconnecting battlements.

We round the point, which juts out like the bow of a ship, at the confluence of the Danube and the Inn. While the hills on the right side of the Danube already belong to Austria, the border on the left bank is still 24 km away. In the Middle Ages, the areas along the Danube all the way to the Hungary Lowlands belonged to the Bishopric of Passau, which was once the largest by area in Germany. Even St. Stephen's Cathedral in Vienna was only an ancillary of the Passau cathedral of the same name, which today is the spiritual centre of Germany's second smallest bishopric.

The main portal of the orphanage.

Passau, the swimming three Rivers City

Because the Inn, on the average, contributes more water annually to the confluence than the Danube does, by rights, the river ought to be called the Inn from Passau on. It was named Danube anyway, probably because the stretch from the source to the confluence is several kilometres longer than the corresponding stretch of the Inn.

Autumn atmosphere at the point. The fortresses Niederhaus and Oberhaus are on the opposite side of the Danube.

The Inn quay is a popular place to walk; in the background, the romantic Schaiblings-tower.

Leaving the park, we approach the handsome **Waisenhaus ("orphanage")** ❺, which today is named Lukas Kern Home for Children after its founder. A likeness of the patriarch and his wife, who herself grew up parentless, and the year „1751" are found above the main entrance. The successful shipowner and brown beer publican left the foundation more than 70,000 guilders with instructions that the house should be used to rear boys and girls (at least twelve each) to „work hard and lead ordered lives". The statue at the entrance recalls „Sterntaler", a well-known fairy tale about an orphan girl.

In the abbey district

Back on the banks of the Inn, we take in the view of the Innstadt district, crowned by the Mariahilf-Kloster (Our Lady of Succour Monastery) above the rooftops. Before us stands one of the city's landmarks, a round tower known as the Schaiblingsturm. In the course of its eventful history, it probably first served, upon completion, as a defensive tower for the landing places of the salt ships and simultaneously as a cutwater. Later, it was used as a magazine for gunpowder and other things.

23

Taking our leave of the Inn promenade in front of the tower, we follow the „Klosterwinkel" along the walls of once-powerful **Niedernburg Abbey** ❻. Founded as a community of cannonesses on the site of a ducal palace in 740, it became an abbey of Benedictine nuns around 1000. The most famous abbess was Queen Gisela, sister of Heinrich II and spouse of King Stephen of Hungary, upon whose death she entered the convent in 1042. The Blessed Gisela's tomb chest in the early Romanesque Heiligkreuz-kirche or „Holy Cross Church" (11th cent.) has attracted countless pilgrims for centuries, and not only from Hungary: likewise, the Gnadenbild „Maria Schütz" (a miracle-working image of the Madonna).

The present-day abbey buildings date from the 14th century and were transferred to the Maria Ward Sisters, also known as the „Institute of English Ladies". They operate two secondary schools here, as well as the Niedernburg Institute. A late Gothic cloister is preserved in the abbey's inner court. The street called Jesuitengasse leads us from Holy Cross Church past the preparatory school in the former Jesuit Seminary and finally, turning left, to the Jesuit Church or Jesuitenkirche (1665-77). This church is dedicated to St. Michael. Plaques on the old patrician houses in Schustergasse inform interested visitors that „an honourable trade in candle making and gingerbread baking was practised here already in 1680", or that Chromy Haus once housed a copper-smith and, from 1886-1972, an office.

Niedernburg Abbey: The tomb of Abbess (and Queen) Gisela.

Open to visitors daily, except during services.

The residence of the bishops

After crossing Schrottgasse/Klaftergasse, Schustergasse finally leads to **Residenzplatz (Residence Square)** ❼. The square is bordered in the north by stately residential buildings, on the south side by the Neue Residenz, the newer palace of the bishops, and on the west side by the Gothic east choir of the Cathedral as well as the Marshall's house which juts forth beside it. The Wittelsbacher Fountain, which was built in the Baroque style in 1903 to commemorate the annexation of Passau to Bavaria one hundred years before, stands in the middle of the square. The column of the fountain is topped by Mary as the Queen of Heaven and patron saint of Bavaria, on whose lap the boy Jesus is seated.

Residenzplatz with the Wittelsbacher Fountain, behind which are seen the Neue Residenz and the Gothic east choir of the cathedral.

25

Three angelic figures at their feet symbolise Passau's three rivers. The figure with the heads of grain in her hair is the Danube, which flows through the fruitful Bavarian alluvial plain. The figure with the pearls in her braids is the Ilz, in which fresh water mussels flourish even today that, in turn, produce valuable pearls. Last but not least, the figure wearing the Tyrolean hat is the Inn, which originates in the Alps. From the fountain, one can also see the patron saint of the church, St. Stephen, who waves his greetings to the sister cathedral in Vienna from a little tower over the roof of the cathedral. The walls of the patrician houses are built in the Italian style, similarly to those on the banks of the Inn (among other things, for reasons of fire prevention), and extend far beyond the eaves. The adjoining Marschallhaus (Marshall's house, façade 1902), which is connected to the cathedral, makes it possible for the present-day bishop to walk from his apartment right into the cathedral, as his predecessors did when they lived in the Neue Residenz. For since 1803, the Neue Residenz has belonged to the Free State of Bavaria, and the bishops (since 1871) have waived their customary right to live in the residence, instead dwelling in the second floor of what was once the office of the seneschal. The building also accommodates a residence for the sexton as well as offices and the church administration. Now that the Neue Residenz has been completely renovated, it is also home to offices of the diocesan administration and the episcopal authorities.

Several houses were demolished to make way for the stretched-out new Baroque edifice called the **Neue Residenz** ❽ (1712-1730). Under Prince Bishop Leopold Ernst von Firmian, who was displeased with the plain building, Melchior Hefele, a student of Balthasar Neumann, undertook to decorate the façade. He is the creator of the two bold balcony por-

Residenzplatz with the Wittelsbach fountain in the foreground.

Wittelsbach fountain.

The Neue Residenz (New Residence) served as the palace of the prince bishops

28

since its completion (1730).

tals and the circular balustrade, both richly decorated with castlead figures, reliefs, and ornaments. They take away the geometrical bleakness of the façade and lend it its present-day early Classical aura. Hefele also created the elaborate Rococo lattice at the court staircase and the representative shaft-type stairwell, which is one of the loveliest in Germany next to the one in the Würzburg palace (Balthasar Neumann). This is contributed to by the fantastic stucco work (Johann Baptist Modler and sons) and the amusing ceiling painting (Johann Georg Unruh: „The Gods of Olympus Protect Immortal Passau"), as well as the charming cherub groups of sculptor Joseph Bergler, who was also responsible for the figures in the façade. The most prominent guest (but not necessarily the most welcome one) was Napoleon Bonaparte, who lodged here in 1809.

On the south side of the cathedral, the Zengergasse connects Residenzplatz with Domplatz. This alleyway has been transversed since the 17th century by a connecting building between the cathedral and the palace, which served as a bridge for the prince bishops between their quarters and the choir of the church. At the right, the Neue Residenz is adjoined by the Saalbau (1575), in which each of the two upper stories is taken up by one room. Since 1989 - following

Neue Residenz: The upper storey of the staircase with varied stucco work and a magnificent ceiling painting.

The splendidly decorated stairway in the Neue Residenz is considered to be one of the loveliest Baroque staircases in Germany.

Ceiling painting.

an eventful history - these rooms house the **Cathedral Treasury and Diocesan Museum** , the basis of which was the collection of Bishop Heinrich von Hofstätter (1839-75). Although most of the medieval utensils in the sacristy were destroyed in the Great Fire of 1662, the treasury was well-filled again by 1792. In 1801, again, most of the holdings were surrendered for war levies in Vienna; the rest were crated up and taken to the new state capital of Munich at the time of secularisation. Some of the older pieces were supposedly preserved for Passau by a local goldsmith who „diverted" one of the crates and its valuable contents and, years later, returned it to the rightful owners. Thus among the prime attractions are the crosiers of the suffragan

bishops Albert Schönhofer (gold-plated, 1490) and Bernhard Meurl (ca. 1520, carved from boxwood). Besides this, the collection includes gold and silver crosses and figures, precious chalices, ciboriums (lidded chalices), diverse reliquaries, monstrances, and much more. Of the few preserved treasures from the Middle Ages, among the most pleasing are a small upright cross (ca. 1470, figures carved from mother-of-pearl), the Bäckerkreuz (Bakers' Cross) (ca. 1480, silver, partly gold-plated), and four figures of saints dating from around 1500. Other things worth seeing, however, include the paintings in the long stretched-out lower hall, which is one of the oldest libraries of its kind in Germany. Both the ceiling painting

Cathedral Treasury and Diocesan Museum:
Beginning May – end Oct. daily 10 AM - 4 PM except Sundays and holidays. Enter through the cathedral and through the Neue Residenz). Guided tours available upon request. Call (0851) 393374.

and the barrel vaulting start just above the bookcases, but visitors are tricked through clever use of perspective into thinking that the room is much higher than it actually is. This trompe l'oeil, which is typical for the Baroque period, was created masterfully by Johann Carlone in 1694 on commission from Cardinal Johann Philipp von Lamberg, whose coat of arms and initials (doubled), next to a coat of arms of the City of Passau, decorate every corner. The sciences of the day, culminating in the-

is closed because of the organ concert, enter through the Neue Residenz. At the level of the choir, the exterior wall of the cathedral is still maintained in the rich decorative forms of the Late Gothic. In the year „1491", just as at Burg Oberhaus, the four is represented as a halved eight. To master the tough task of integrating the Gothic façade in the Baroque new construction, cathedral architect Carlo Lurago used wall panels that divided the high lancet windows into a low round arch and an oval. From the

The hall library.

ology, are depicted as allegorical figures. In the central ceiling medallion, Apollo is portrayed amidst the muses, winged Pegasus is also seen in the background. The second room of the museum above the library, the Great Court Hall, was decorated in Baroque style in 1730. During opening hours (see info block, p. 22), the Cathedral Treasury and the Diocesan Museum are reached through the cathedral. Between 10:45 am and 12:30 pm, however, when the cathedral

colours of the blocks, one can clearly see where the sandstone had to be torn out and replaced during the last renovation because of damage during the Great Fire. In Zengergasse, we make our way to a column-flanked portal with two coats-of-arms and a bust. According to the information board right behind the entrance, the old prince bishop's residence was first mentioned in 1173 and was named in 1188 as „Palatium bataviense". Extensions and fortifications around

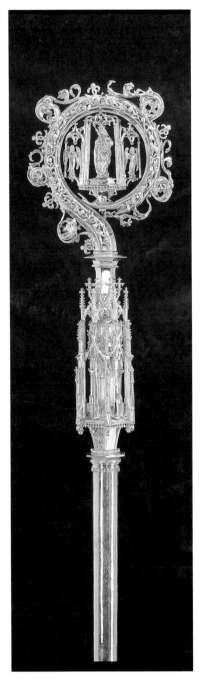

Crosier of the suffragan Bishop Bernhard Meurl († 1526), elaborately carved out of boxwood.

Late Gothic, gold-plated bishop's crosier (15th cent.)

34

Candle holder in the shape of a little man, ca. 1400.

1350 and before 1450 (inclusion of the Innbrücktor and the Zengerhof) caused the palace to grow into a sprawling complex and are still recognisable in the modern fabric of the building. These include the Gothic Hofkapelle (Court Chapel) (1491-93), typical construction elements of which are preserved in the inner court.

Due to the riches of the prince bishops, founded above all on the salt trade, the Old Residence was magnificently furnished according to the standards of the time and often hosted Emperors, Kings, and even a Pope: Heinrich III and Pope Leo IX (1052), Heinrich IV (1058 and 1063), Frederick Barbarossa (1065 and

Gold-plated monstrance, crafted ca. 1670 by Hans Franz Fesenmayer (Augsburg).

1072), Frederick II (1217), Rudolf von Habsburg (1276), Frederick III (1444), Karl V (1532), and Kings Ferdinand I and Ferdinand II (1552 and 1630 respectively). One of the societal high points was the wedding of Emperor Leopold I and Princess Eleonora von Pfalz-Neuburg, which was held in 1676 in the court chapel. This event is depicted, among other places, as a fresco in the Great Assembly Room at Town Hall. When the Turks laid siege to Vienna in 1683, Emperor Leopold and his entire Imperial Government repaired to the prince bishop's residence. It was here that they com-

missioned the „Saviour of the Occident", Prince Eugene of Savoy, as the general of their army. With his consort, by the way, Leopold fathered ten children, one of whom became Emperor of Germany as Karl VI. He, in turn, fathered the later empress Maria Theresa, who herself bore sixteen children and had 18 grandchildren from just one of her daughters. Since power politics made marriage to commoners virtually impossible, it is no wonder that the royal houses of Europe were often interrelated. The Habsburgers were especially known for cleverly arranged political marriages.

Domplatz: the west façade of Passau's Stephansdom (Cathedral of Saint Stephen). In the foreground: a monument to King Maximillian I Joseph, King of Bavaria.

The Stephansdom (Saint Stephen's Cathedral) ❿

Exiting the alley, which is named after a Passau canon, through the bottom of the south tower, we step out onto the broad cathedral square. The statue was a gift of the people to King Maximilian I Joseph on the 25th anniversary of his reign on 16 February, 1824. He was the grandfather of Empress Elisabeth (Sissi) of Austria and great-grandfather of the „fairy-tale king" Ludwig II, the builder of Neuschwanstein. The Elector and (as of 1806, by the grace of Napoleon) first King of Bavaria is depicted with outstretched arm and is thus popularly known as the „rain-tester". From here we cast a look at the west façade, which is

Guided tours: *May - Oct., daily at 2:30 PM, Mondays – Saturdays (except Holidays) also at 10:30 AM, Nov. - April daily at 12.15 PM, duration 1 hour, meeting point: cathedral portal.*

<– The Cathedral of St. Stephen: A view through the nave toward the organ loft. At right: the gilt pulpit.

dominated by twin towers with Baroque cupolas (68 m). The three-story tower was built from scratch in 1674/75; the octagonal additions, however, were only added in the late 19th century. The middle tower (which is 1 meter higher) on the other hand, emerged from the Great Fire of 1662 largely unscathed and was merely fitted with a matching cupola as a concession to the Baroque design. The bells were lost along with the twin towers and replacements had to be cast. Thus, the oldest 5300kg bell of the present-day set, the "Stürmerin", was cast in Passau in 1733, whilst the heaviest bell, the "Pummerin", was created here in 1952 and weighs 7550 kg. In the Christmas season of 1999 the cathedral received its eighth bell, the second heaviest "Misericordia", weighing in at 6000kg. The bells harmonise well despite the differences in their ages and are often heard throughout Germany via radio and television broadcasts. Starting in 1709, the west façade was extended by the addition of a mausoleum for Cardinal Johann Philipp von Lamberg, which was adapted to the façade of the cathedral. A soldiers' monument on the exterior wall commemorates the 16th Royal Bavarian Infantry Regiment and Passavians killed in action during World War I. On the left,

today the building is connected to the Seminary of St. Max. It served first of all as a seminary and priests' residence, then, from 1843 until 1983, as a school that prepared young men for religious vocations. Parts of the 14th century Gothic cloister are preserved in the cathedral court, including the Andreas (1320), Ortenburg (1350) and Trenbach (1572) Chapels. From notes made by Eugippius in the year 511, we learn that there was already a church with a baptismal chapel in Passau in the times of St. Severinus (died 482). A second document (from ca. 635) mentions a „Church of Saint Stephen within the city walls". In the year 731, at the latest, there is verification of the existence of a church that was an official bishop's see and which Vivilo, the first bishop of Passau, discovered upon arrival. When Saint Bonifatius came to Passau in 739 on a visitation tour on behalf of the Pope, it remained only for him to confirm the existing bishopric, and the church became the Diocesan Cathedral of St. Stephen. When the relics of St. Valentine, who later became patron saint of the bishopric, were transferred to Passau (764), it became even more important. The bishopric expanded along the Danube as far as the Hungarian Lowlands and became

Cathedral Opening Hours:
daily from 6:30 AM till 7 PM at summertime and 6 PM at wintertime. At days when there is a concert at noon it is closed from 10.45 AM till 12.30 AM. At days when there is an evening concert from 6 PM on.
Cathedral tours: *May - October, workdays at 12:30 PM. Meeting point: cathedral portal.*
Organ concerts on the world's largest cathedral-organ in the Cathedral of St. Stephen:
Concerts at noon: *May - October during Advent every wed. and sat., during the Christmas holidays, workdays Noon - 12:30 PM. doors open at 11:20 AM. Tickets are available at day of the concert from 10 AM in the Cathedral.*
Concerts in the evening: *May - October every Thursday, except on holidays 7:30 PM, doors open at 6.45 PM. Tickets are available at day of the concert from 6:30 PM in the Cathedral. There are no concerts on Sundays and holidays, but the organ is played during the 7:30, 9:30 and 11:30 AM masses.*

the largest by area in any German-speaking nation. The church was damaged when Emperor Otto II besieged and took the city by storm in 977, so under Bishop Pilgrim the church was rebuilt in early Romanesque style. The three-naved cathedral, consecrated in 985,

were moved here; from this point on, St. Maximillian had the function of a second diocesan patron saint in addition to Saint Valentine. Under prince bishop Wernhard von Prambach (starting 1284), the longest phase of construction on the cathedral commenced, including recon-

Fresco on the drum of the cupola with the figure of God the Father, encircled by his angelic hosts.

the site of the presentday cathedral and was just as big, if one disregards the late-Gothic chancel and the Baroque west façade. On the occasion of the consecration, the relics of St. Maximillian

struction in Gothic style (until around 1390) and rebuilding and expansion in late-Gothic fashion, which was finally completed in 1570. The long construction period is not anomalous for a Gothic church, and it's no surprise when one beholds the rich structure, especially the exterior walls with the towers and turrets. When Wenzeslaus von Thun, the dean of the cathedral, became bishop of Passau two years after the Great Fire of 1662, he settled on an up-to-date baroque edifice instead of the previously intended reconstruction of the late-Gothic cathedral. After making preliminary plans on his own and securing funding through a partly levied, partly begged „Cathedral Construction Fund", the prince bishop engaged the Italian builder Carlo Lurago to realise his designs. Lurago's task was to integrate the late-Gothic parts of the east choir – the choir, transept, and crossing tower, and the north wall of the nave up to the cloister – in his baroque reconstruction, which he succeeded in doing superbly. He took a new path in creating the vaults: In the naive, he created flat, elliptical cupolas between the reinforcing arches; by virtue of the removal of the crossbeam system, the cupola of the choir became a uniform decorative field measuring 214 m² just by itself. In 1677, the stucco worker Giovanni Battista Carlone was commissioned to do all the stucco work in the 102 m long, 33 m wide and nearly 30 m high house of God. It took him and his up to 13 workers 17 years to decorate the surfaces and create the 10 side altars. During this time, a singular composition of opulent fullness emerged, clear and lucid and never repetitive. Conspicuous among the elements from the plant world, created with almost limitless fantasy, is the corn cob, which is known in the local dialect as a „carlon". These ornaments are joined by around 1000 stucco figures such as prophets up to 4.2 m tall, figures of Atlas holding up beams, allegorical female figures and troops of cherubs holding banners with sayings. The sayings bear witness to the spirit of the Counter-Reformation, which imbued the prince bishops in those days. Just two years after work on the stuccoes began, the then already well-known painter Carpoforo Tencalla began painting the vault surfaces, of which there are 171 in all. When the cathedral and the wooden scaffolding caught fire a second time, in 1680, part of his works and the stucco work itself were damaged and required painstaking restoration. In the process, the artist painted over remnants of some older paintings. In one of the new paintings, one can still see a stray hand that Tencalla overlooked, probably that of the supervising architect Lurago, holding the plans of the cathedral. Instead, Tencalla painted himself and Lurago again very inconspicuously in the 155 m² choir fresco, although the figures are still easy to identify because of their fashionable Baroque clothing. Another oddity is the attempt made in some places to lend a three-dimensional look to body parts through added pieces, a technique that was frequently applied in later years. After Tencalla's death

Gilt pulpit (18th cent.), crowned by the church personified in Ecclesia.

Modern high altar with a representation of the stoning of St. Stephen.

(1685), it took another three years, to finish the entire work. The cathedral came through much of the Second World War unscathed, but on May 2, 1945, direct hits from artillery, followed by inrushing water, damaged the painted decorations. Through extensive restoration 1972-80, however, it was possible to return the artworks to their original condition. Thus today, the cathedral offers visitors a complete artwork, in which Baroque architecture, stuccoes, and painting harmonise exquisitely. A typical example of this is the central cupola, flooded with light, featuring a depiction of the Christian heaven with God the Father seated on his throne, surrounded by the heavenly hosts. Here as well, two angels let their legs dangle from the picture out into the room. On the paintings beneath the cupola, several prince bishops of Passau are portrayed with the regalia of their office, the crosier for the spiritual and the sword for the temporal authority. We can recognise their rank by the colour of their clothing and the associated cross: Those dressed in red and with the double crossbeam in the cross are cardinals; the others are just „plain" bishops. The bishop's loge on the south side of the choir, which is connected directly to the residence, was built for them all. Today, one can reach the Cathedral Treasury and the Diocesan Museum in the New Residence this way. The striking furnishings of the cathedral include the all-gilt pulpit carved out of basswood, a costly Vienna creation dating from 1720. In this technique, the gold is beaten until it is so thin that 1 g of gold yields approx. 2 m^2 of gold leaf. In addition to allegorical figures, the four evangelists are portrayed on the body of the chancel; the canopy bears a likeness of Ecclesia, the symbol of the Christian church, with the globe and the light of revelation in the form of a church steeple.

The cases of three of the five organs which, taken together, form the largest church organ in the world, also date from the first half of the 18th century. The moving casing of the gigantic great organ bears the Lamberg coat-of-arms and hides both the largest (11.30 m long and 47 cm in diameter) and smallest (6 mm long) pipes. The cases of the two organs in the aisles, the epistle organ and the gospel organ, are similarly designed. They are supplemented by the choir organ (case built 1978) and the „echo organ", which is tucked away above the middle of the naive between the vaulting and the roof. Its muted tones reach the interior through the „Holy Spirit hole" in the vaulting, where, in centuries past, the wooden or stucco figure of a dove referred to the sending of the Holy Spirit. Since being rebuilt and expanded in the seventies by a Passau company specialised in such work, the entire organ contains 17,974 pipes and 233 ringing registers. More than 120 km of cable had to be laid in the attic so that all the organs can be played from one console at the same time. From May until the end of October and between Christmas and New Year's Day, visitors can experience the tonal sensation of the world's largest church organ not only on Sundays and holidays

The moving casing of the gigantic great organ bears the Lamberg coat-of-arms and hides both the largest and smallest pipes.

Imaginative stuccoes and paintings decorate the vaulting of the nave. To the

right and left in the foreground are cherubs holding scrolls.

at mass, but also workdays between noon and 12.30 (an admission fee is charged). For this reason, the cathedral is closed to sightseers from 11 o'clock until the end of the organ concert. Furthermore, during the aforementioned season, there is also an organ concert every Thursday (except on holidays) at 7:30 PM, which occasionally also takes the form of a sacred concert with choir, soloists, and orchestra. There is an artwork of our century here that still deserves our attention: the altar, created 1947-53 by Professor Henselmann of Munich. Fashioned from poplar wood and lined with silver-plated copper sheeting, it refers to a theme that is also of topical interest, namely violence against and brutality toward minorities. The altar shows Saint Stephen, the first Christian martyr, being stoned by his fellow human beings, and his vision at the hour of his death: „I see the heavens opening and the Son of Man standing at the right hand of God." In the early Middle-Ages, the bishops were buried in the crypt. Little attention was paid to the crypt after the church went over to interring bishops' remains in the sanctuary itself, starting in the 13th century. In 1678, however, under the direction of Lurages, the vault of the prince bishops under the choir was rebuilt and has since served as the resting place of Passau's bishops. The faithful are only permitted to visit their metal sarcophagi after the pontifical requiem on All Saints' / All Souls' Day and on the anniversary of the death of the most recently deceased bishop. The tombstones, however, were erected in the sanctuary, started with the tombstone of the first bishop to die after reconstruction, Wenzel von Thun (died 1673) in the choir, and ended yet with Antonius Hofman, (died 2000) in the southern aisle. Moreover, the pillars hold memorial plaques for those bishops who were not interred in the cathedral.

From the cathedral square back to town hall

Bishop Konrad von Babenberg reserved the area of the cathedral square, including the adjoining property, for the chapter of the cathedral in 1155: Here the canons built their palace over hundreds of years, so that, at times, the place was also called Pfaffenhof or „Priests' Court". Lamberg Palace (Lambergpalais), the only edifice of its kind still in existence, was built in Rococo style in 1724. It stands on the west side of the square, which was first opened to the public upon secularisation in 1803. Just behind the regional court complex, a narrow alley named Carlonegasse (after the Italian family of artists) leads toward the Inn. Turning off half-way to the right, it takes us to Grabengasse, which was once the western limit of the old town. Today, it is part of Passau's pedestrian precinct and shopping area, a magnet for out-of-towners and locals alike. A few hundred meters and many interesting shops later, we reach Ludwigstraße, which constitutes the main axis of the shopping district. We follow it – opposite the main direction – to the right to the Rindermarkt („beef market"). A plaque to the left commemorates

A flautist in Carlonegasse.

Shopping in the pedestrian precinct in front of the Spitalkirche (15th cent.).

the medieval Spital or hospital which, according to tradition, was located here outside the city wall from ca. 1200 on. The present-day edifice of the Spitalkirche St. Johann (St. John's Church) originated in the 14th/15th centuries. It's only just a few meters from here to the far bigger **Church of Saint Paul** ⓫, which stands right next to the „Paulusbogen". The Paulusbogen or „Arch of Paul" is the oldest of the five extant gates to the city, and simultaneously provides access to the old town at the former Roman wall. From here the Steinweg, Passau's first paved street, leads toward the

Large winged altar-piece in the Spitalkirche.

View from Rindermarkt of the Baroque Church of St. Paul and the Paulusbogen.

Statue of St. Paul at the front façade of the Church of St. Paul.

cathedral. But first of all, let us take a look at the inside of the parish church, which was preceded by Romanesque (1050) and Gothic-style buildings. A new, Baroque-style church stood on this site already in 1678, just 16 years after the Great Fire. Since the church and parish were assigned to the chapter of the cathedral in 1179, the master builder of the cathedral also took charge of planning and execution here. Unlike the cathedral, here the builders dispensed with frescoes and statues, so that the focus is all the more on the furnishings – especially the altars which provide an effective contrast to the white wall surfaces. The main altar extends all the way up into the vaulting.

The structure made of black-stained wood is adorned with gilt ornaments and eleven figures; some of the figures are even in colour. The gigantic main picture shows the beheading of St. Paul, a masterful work painted by Franz Werner Tamm around 1700. The contrasts are especially impressive: muted colours in the execution scene, bright ones in the opening heavens. Between the pairs of Corinthian columns are larger-than-life statues of the apostles Peter and Andrew. Even the oval upper picture depicting Mary as the mother of God is 2.50 m high. Above it, with his head almost touching the vaulting, is

The Church of St. Paul: The high altar towers above the two side altars. The altar-piece painting (the beheading of St. Paul) is flanked by statues of Sts. Peter and Andrew.

Christ triumphant, holding the globe in his left hand. The altar-table, gilt tabernacle, and halo were added later. The side altars are designed very similarly, even if on a somewhat more modest scale. The organ cases and the pulpit also stick to the prescribed colour scheme, predominantly black and gold. As in the cathedral, the four evangelists are portrayed on the body of the pulpit, the four fathers of the church on the canopy. Of the few surviving tombstones, the tombstone of the Kerns,

the couple already mentioned above, is especially noteworthy. To the right and left of the epitaph with the history of the family, the institutions they founded are also depicted; the most important of these, the orphanage, is above the writing. Another epitaph commemorates the Braguia family, who also bequeathed a vast fortune to ecclesiastical and social institutions. An exceptionally large votive picture shows the second Great Fire of the 17th century, when, just 18 years after the worst catas-

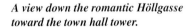

Atmospheric old town alleys lead down to the banks of the Danube.

A view down the romantic Höllgasse toward the town hall tower.

trophe (1662), flames swept through the city anew. Fortunately, the 1680 fire spared the just-completed Church of St. Paul, whereupon the parish priest at the time had the picture painted. Of even greater artistic value, however, is the devotional picture „Lamentation of Mary" (1689) by Johann Michael Rottmayer. After painting the first version (which is now part of the art collection of the state of Bavaria), the artist painted a second, similar version. The foreground is dominated by Christ's corpse, which rests in the lap of his mother after having been taken down from the cross.

After leaving the Church of St. Paul, we follow Steinweg for awhile until we turn off to the left, descending through the picturesque Schlosserstiege to **Höllgasse** ⓬. Now we follow this alley - parallel to the Danube - back to the square at town hall. Along the way we cross the romantic alleyways of the old town, such as Pfaffengasse („Priests' Alley") - which was once the street where the cathedral preacher lived - and the Kleine Messergasse („Little Knife-Alley"). This street name commemorates an elaborate craft native to Passau, that of the bladesmith. Until the 18th century, daggers and swords

51

An elaborate cantilever at the Hotel „Wilder Mann".

branded with the Passau wolf were every bit as famous as those made of Damascus steel or made in Toledo, and were imitated by, among others, the competing city of Solingen with a phoney wolf. The famous painters Rueland Frueauf the Elder and Rueland Frueauf the Younger also lived in this alley around 1500. Even today, the alley is well-known as the quarter where various artisans live and work, some of whom even occasionally permit tourists to look over their shoulders while they are at work. At the end of Höllgasse, several patrician houses each were combined to form a complex within the framework of an exemplary old town renewal program. On the right side, we see the four Baroque buildings, still maintained in their original condition, which were combined to form the Hotel „Wilder Mann". In the 19th century, „Wilder Mann", which operated on a smaller scale then, was the most prestigious hotel in the city. Those who have lodged here include, among others: the Austrian novelist Adalbert Stifter, the 19th century Prussian general Graf von Moltke, airship inventor Graf Zeppelin, and, in 1985, ex-astronaut Neil Armstrong, the first man to set foot on the moon. All these celebrities, however, were outstripped by the eight-day visit of Empress Elisabeth of Austria, popularly known as Sissi, who met here in September 1862 with her parents, Duke Max and Duchess Ludowika of Bavaria, and her sister Marie, the Queen of Bourbon-Naples.

Although the royal guests had prohibited all receptions, Passau natives couldn't be discouraged from paying their respects to the royals by holding a torch-light pro-

cession and presenting music and songs. This spectacle also made it evident that Passau's residents felt more attached to Austria than to Bavaria at the time. Even today, romantically inclined guests can lodge in „Empress Sissi's bedroom", feast in the evening at the celebrated gourmet restaurant „Kaiserin Sissi" or admire the largest German-language collection of cookbooks (the earliest date from 1450), 11,800 volumes in all, which is housed in the Imperial Halls.

The **Passau Glass Museum** ⓭ was opened on March 15, 1985 by Neil Armstrong, the first man on the moon.

> **Friedrich Dürrenmatt called the Passau Glass Museum " the world's most beautiful glass house".**

Exhibit in the Biedermeier Hall: Glassware from the Baroque to Historicism.

Passau Glass Museum am Rathausplatz
(town-hall square): Open daily 9 am - 6 pm.
Phone (0851) 35 071.

Baroque and Rococo 1700-1800.   *Empire 1800-1830.*

Biedermeier and second Rococo 1825-1860.   *Historicism 1860-1900.*

The Passau Glass Museum is housed in the historic "Wilder Mann" building complex on Rathausplatz in the middle of Passau's downtown historical district. It is home to the world's largest collection of Bohemian glass.

Over 30,000 items of glassware, 15,000 of which are on display, offer a comprehensive summary of the various epochs of glassmaking. Exhibits on four floors give visitors a lively look at 250 years of glassmaking history from 1700 to 1950, running the gamut of Baroque, Rococo, Empire, Biedermeier, Historicism, Art-Nouveau, Art-Deco and Modern styles. The focus of the collection is on the 19th Century up until the Art-Nouveau period. The Passau Glass Museum is on the list of "National Cultural Treasures".

54

Art Nouveau 1900-1915.

Quote regarding the Passau Glass Museum

"Some 80 % of the art objects produced by the Bohemian glassworks have fallen victim to the winds of war and barbarianism as well as human ignorance. It is thus all the more remarkable that the largest unified collection of Bohemian glassware is preserved in Passau, point of departure for the one-time Golden Path to Bohemia. I have seen many glass collections all over the world, but nothing compares to this."

(Prince Karl von Schwarzenberg)

Art-Deco and Modern 1915-1950.

Publications

In four years of teamwork, fifteen glass experts from Austria, the Czech Republic, and Germany have compiled a unique standard guide to Bohemian glass, published by Passau Glass Museum in seven volumes with a total of 1184 pages and 1606 illustrations, entitled "Das böhmische Glas 1700 bis 1950" (Georg Höttl, editor).

The citadel Veste Oberhaus 14

The shuttle bus is the most comfortable way to get from the Rathausplatz (Town Hall Square) to the former citadel of the prince bishops 108 m above the city (departs every 30 minutes from Palm Sunday through October). The bus stops directly in the castle courtyard, while cars must park in the parking lot above the castle. Parking is free of charge. To get to the fortress by car, drive across the Schanzlbrücke and then follow the signs at the bridgehead leading to the driveway. Alternatively, you can drive across the suspension bridge, follow the signs for Freyung, take the first left across the second Ilz bridge, and then turn right at the second street up to the hill (for cars only). If you're feeling fit and are up to a hike, we can recommend an interesting route: cross the suspension bridge and follow the footpath which starts directly opposite

the north bridgehead with the first of 200 steps, blasted out of the rock in 1893 and dubbed „Ludwigsteig" (Ludwig's Footpath). Further up the stairs, the path takes you through the battlements connecting the Veste Oberhaus and Veste Niederhaus. Please note that the path closes at 5 PM, however. After Kaiser Frederick II invested Bishop Ulrich with the title of Imperial Prince in 1217, the prince began with the construction of the castle grounds. The castle also protected the prince bishops when the peasants revolted against their rule, for instance, in 1367, when the residents of Passau unsuccessfully laid siege to the fortress. In the later part of the 16th century, the prince bishops expanded the fortress into a national citadel and continued modernising it. Around 1700, a star-shaped peripheral rampart was erected. In 1803, Bavaria also took possession of the expanded stronghold as a national citadel

(until 1867). From 1822 until 1918, the citadel served as a Bavarian military prison. When the city of Passau took possession of the buildings, they were allocated new functions. Today, they are home to a youth hostel and a meteorological observation station. The Veste Oberhaus, however, is taken up mostly by the largest city museum in Lower Bavaria. A total of 3000 m² of attractively designed exhibits brings the history of the cathedral-city to life, from the Middle Ages to the present. Among its most supraregionally significant exhibits are „White Gold", documenting Passau's position as the most important salt-trading city in the region of present-day Bavaria, „The Secret of the Brotherhood", documenting Passau's guilds and skilled trades, and the outstanding collection of Gothic and Baroque Passau artwork featuring masterpieces by local painters and wood carvers. Located next to this in the Veste

The "Veste Oberhaus" stands at the confluence of the Ilz and Danube Rivers.

The buildings of the Veste Oberhaus, which boasts almost 800 years of history, have a curiously modern look about them.

Oberhaus, you can visit the Bohemian Forest Museum and see exhibits on the history of fire departments in Lower Bavaria, Passau porcelain, Passau apothecaries, and the Hans Wimmer Collection featuring works of one of the most significant German sculptors of the 20th century. The exhibition "The Fascinating Middle Ages" offers realistic insights into the lives and thinking of people in the Middle Ages. Spectacular objects, precious works of art, and important artifacts uncovered by excavation give visitors a feel for the past. The varying special exhibitions are a special attraction and draw many visitors.

There are numerous interesting signboards with the names and dates of completion or use on the building themselves: the Brückenturm (bridge tower, 14th cen-

tury), the Zeughaus (the arsenal), the Kommandantur (commander's office), and the Trenbachbau: Duke Ernst of Bavaria turned this last building, formerly a guesthouse, into the „Tollhaus" („madhouse") – as the mental institution was referred to back then. Close to the museum, there is also one of the most magnificent views of Passau, the Three-Rivers View. From here, directly across the suspension bridge, one has the best view of the rivers and their different colours: the Ilz with its dark water from the fens of the Bavarian Forest and the Inn with its light green torrents form a stark contrast to the famous „blue" Danube. The Veste Niederhaus (13th century), once inhabited by Passau's historical painter Ferdinand Wagner is situated at the confluence of

Oberhaus Museum: www.oberhausmuseum.de
April – Beginning of Nov. Mo-Fr 9 AM-5 PM, Sa, Su & Holidays 10 AM-6 PM
Shuttle bus service between the fortress and Rathausplatz,
End of March till beginning of November Mo - Fr 10 AM – 5 PM, Sa, Su & Bank Holidays 10 AM - 6 PM.

Oberhausmuseum: Salt trade

the Ilz and Danube. It is privately owned to this day and is therefore not open for public viewing. Opposite the Three-River Corner on the other side of the Danube is Austrian territory, while the border on the left bank of the river is 24 km downstream. Visitors also have a nice view of the city and surrounding region from the Aussichtsturm (observation tower) and from a broad terrace outside the courtyard.

In the museum.

Historical representations of river trips from earlier centuries: towing and drifting.

Castle life: the panel painting "The Annunciation of Mary" (ca. 1468) offers a glimpse inside a bedroom.

View from the three-rivers vantage point of the confluence of the dark Ilz

(foreground) and the bright Inn (rear) with the waters of the Danube.

In the Ilzstadt

To descend into the narrow Ilz Valley, either drive or walk down Ferdinand-Wagner-Straße. Close to the outer wall between the two fortresses is the former **Wallfahrtskirche St. Salvator (Pilgrimage Church of St. Salvator)**  at Platz der Synagoge (Synagogue Square). The synagogue was destroyed during the 1476 pogrom. The Christian church was erected 1479-1570 as „atonement". The pogrom was the result of the alleged „Desecration of Hosts", supposedly staged by the Jews living in Ilzstadt. They allegedly took a knife and stabbed consecrated hosts stolen from the church, whereupon blood began flowing from the sacramental bread. After this incident, more than 100 stories of similar occurrences circulated throughout the Occident. The towerless Gothic structure is presently used as a concert hall.

The passages for the street tunnels leading to Ilzstadt, on the other hand, are of more recent origin. the eastern passage was created in 1762, the western one in 1948, both of them were widened to accommodate two-lane traffic in 1979. The **Veste Niederhaus** ⓰ is situated at the end of the rock barrier at the mouth of the Ilz. Parts of its wall still rest on the exposed rock. Originally erected in 1255, the present structure dates from sometime after 1435. Since the former castle is privately owned, our view of it ends at the gate bearing the coat of arms. Both castles also served as protection for the salt trade which was the major basis of Passau's wealth. Ilzstadt used to be the starting point of an overland route into saltless Bohemia, called the „Golden Path" due to the profitable prospects for merchants who used the route. The merchants reloaded salt and products from Italy onto their pack animals and transported the goods towards Freyung and Waldkirchen. More than 3000 packhorses a week covered the route. Each horse could carry up to 1.5 hundredweights. They hauled salt, tropical fruits, wine, oil, spices, and paper into Bohemia and returned with grain, malt, hops, spirits, animal hides, and wool. The „Säumertor" („Pack Gate"), renovated in 1983, is a reminder of the height of prosperity of the once independent Ilzstadt, where pack vassals, blacksmiths, packers, and loading vassals all once made a living. Lumberjacks and log-driving vassals, responsi-

Captivating reflection of the spireless Salvatorkirche in the dark waters of the Ilz.

The Veste Niederhaus at the mouth of the Ilz has the appearance of a moated castle.

ble for floating the logs down the river, fishers, bargemen, and craftsmen also lived here. The old Romantic riverbank structures along the Danube recently had to make way for a flood-safe, but dull, row of houses. A visit to the plain parish church of St. Bartholomäus is more worthwhile. The Romanesque tower of the former structure is still intact.

A foot path leads from the parking lot next to the cemetery to the Klosterberg (Cloister Hill) where the „Salvatorians" have lived according to the rules of their order since 1925. Here, hikers can enjoy another magnificent view of the „floating city" from above.

View of the Innkai from the Inn-brücke with the defiant Schaiblings-turm. To the left, imposing Jesuit buildings: St. Michael's Church and the former Seminary.

A stroll through the Innstadt district

Leaving Residenzplatz (Residence Square) through a wrought-iron portal brings us to the Neue Residenz (New Residence). From there, go down the „Hofstiege" („Courtyard Stairs") to Innbrückgasse and continue along. You can see the wellfortified Innbrückbogen (Inn Bridge Arch) which, as early as the 12th century, formed the city-side bridge-head of the first wooden bridge (1143). It provides only minimal room for modern traffic. To the right, the façade of the Residence facing the Inn adjoins with the former **Prince-Bishop's Opera House** ❼ (1783), which presently houses the City Theatre. The bridge, with the prominent Schaiblingsturm in the background,

Italian-style structures in the Innbrückgasse.

The former prince bishop opere house. Today, the city theatre.

View from the Innpromenade of the city on the Inn with the parish church of St. Gertraud and the Mariahilf-Kloster.

View from the Innpromenade to the Pilgrims' Stairs and the convent Mariahilf.

separates Passau's most popular promenades, the tree-shaded Innpromenade and the Innkai („Inn Quay"), known as such due to its Italian-style design. **The parish church of St. Gertraud** 🔟, is visible on the other riverbank. It

Pilgrim praying near the top of the Pilgrims' Stairs, which is decorated with numerous votive pictures.

was built on the location of the medieval Spitalkirche (Hospital Church) in 1815 (tower, 1855). Most of the former furnishings were lost in the Great Fire of Innstadt in 1809. The only thing of interest left to see inside is the „Severinsmadonna". This life-size carved statue portrays the crowned Madonna, standing on the crescent of the moon holding her son in both hands in front of her. This brilliant statue was created around 1450 and is one of the finest examples of much-acclaimed Passau sculpture. Diagonally opposite, on the corner of Kirchenplatz / Ledergasse, a façade decorated with numerous eagles and other figures stands out. The building was mentioned in a document from 1552 as the „Elephant House" and, functioning as a Spanish embassy building in 1683, accommodated Prince Eugen of Savoy, the famed army commander of the imperial forces who fought against the Turks in the battle of Vienna and the Occident. Since 1720, it bears the name of „Eagle House" (Haus der Adler). In extension of the Innbrücke, Mariahilfbergstraße leads up to the **pilgrimage church of Mariahilf**

19 (upper parking lot). Pedestrians should turn left at Römerstraße. It runs along the old city wall, still intact in some places. One of its peel towers is still occupied to this day (Römerstr. 4). At Kapuzinerplatz (Capuchin Square), you come to the through street leading to the border crossing Achleiten im Donautal. The square and Kapuzinerstraße, which begins here, are named after the religious order which Baron Marquard von Schwendi, founder of the pilgrimage church, summoned to Passau in 1616. With the help of generous benefactors and using his own resources,

The pilgrimage church of Mariahilf (1624-1627) became famous throughout Germany in 1683 after Emperor Leopold I prayed here for victory over the Turkish forces who had besieged Vienna.

Pilgrimage church: View of the Baroque main altar with the Miracle-Working Image of the Madonna. In the foreground, the „Kaiserampel", donated in 1676 by Kaiser Leopold I on the occasion of his wedding in Passau.

the cathedral dean erected a monastery with a church for the Capuchins and entrusted them with the pastoral care for the pilgrimage church on the hill, documented in his founder's letter of 1631.

From 1622-1628, he had two sets of wooden stairs (Wallfahrtsstiege) built, making the church accessible for pilgrims. The „Sacred Stairs" were reserved for the monks, the „worldly" ones were for the pilgrims. Upon secularisation under Napoleon I in 1803, the monastery was closed and later demolished. The church and the stairs also went to ruins. Bishop Heinrich von Holstetter was the first to revive the pilgrimages in the middle of the 19th century. He is responsible for the construction of the present covered Pilgrims' Stairs leading upwards from Kapuzinerplatz. There are 321 steps in all leading up to Mariahilfberg. The steps are filed with pilgrims climbing in prayer. The reconstruction of the stairs also included the installation of the stations of the cross in 1864. As you will notice, the further up you go, the more votive pictures with messages of gratitude from the faithful you see. At the top, go through the gate into the courtyard of the monastery. The surrounding buildings are mostly from Schwendi's time. The founder we mentioned previously, who was a canon (starting in 1594), the cathedral dean (1612), and the bishopric administrator (1626-1634) in Passau, had a wooden chapel built on this spot based on divine visions he had in 1622. For the veneration of Mary, he had a Madonna added to the altar. The Madonna is a copy of a masterpiece by Lucas Cranach the Elder. However, the throngs of pilgrims were so overwhelming that the founder decided to lay the foundation stone for the present pilgrimage church just two years later. All the buildings were completed by 1630, as you can see from the inscriptions on many buildings on the north side. The building opposite, the Administratur, is the only one that was built later, in 1812 as the Mesnerhaus (Sexton House). The former market booths on the south side were converted into niches with reliefs in 1846. There is a small cemetery in the southeast corner of the courtyard, next to an archway bearing the date 1628. It serves as the final resting place for the Capuchin monks who were summoned back to their former home in 1864. Outside of the archway, you can still see remains of the earthen breastworks constructed by Napoleon in 1809. He had plans to turn Passau into his first fortress, even at the cost of sacrificing the pilgrimage church. Fortunately, he decided against carrying out his plans after a visit here. The structure to the north of the cemetery, the „Alte Hospiz", serves the order as a monastery today. In a niche on the ground floor of the south tower, there is a representation of Blessed Virgin Mary, her mother, St. Anne, and the Christ child (from 1627); above the main portal is Mary, the Queen of Heaven, lifting up a kneeling pilgrim in a benevolent gesture. The inscription below tells of the crisis when Turkish forces had besieged Vienna and threatened the entire Occident: „In 1683 at this spot, Kaiser Leopold I, accompanied by the saintly Capuchin Father Markho, beseeched the help of God for victory over the Ottomans at Vienna." The ensuing triumph imparted the pilgrimage of Mariahilf and the miracle-working image such prestige that, in 1738, the number of Holy Communions totalled 125,000 (compared to a total of 36,000 per year at present). The pilgrims back then came all the way from the Lower Rhine, Upper Italy, and Hungary, and the image of the Madonna was referred to as „Das deutsche Gnadenbild" („The German Miracle-Working Image"). The interior of the early Baroque church makes a plain impression, as prescribed in the ordinance for the churches of mendicant orders. This makes the colourful and gold-plated elements of the furnishings stand out all the more: the statues, the glass display cases with votive boards and gifts, and Turkish weapons (trophies from the Battle of Vienna), the side altars, and especially the Baroque high altar with the Miracle-Working Image in the centre, supported by angels. Aside from numerous other figures of angels, you can see the Saints of the Plague, St. Rochus (showing a

Two angels hold the Miracle-Working Image with an Image of the Madonna (a copy, the original is from Lukas Cranach the Elder), crowned with a baldachin.

bubo sore) and St. Sebastian (riddled with arrows). They remind us of the Scourge of Mankind of former times. The Passau region was last afflicted with the Plague in 1634. The most valuable piece of art in the church, however, is the „Kaiserampel" („Imperial Lamp"), donated by Kaiser Leopold I on the occasion of his marriage to Countess Eleonora in 1676 and crafted by Lukas Lang in Augsburg.

Today the former sacristy serves as a museum and houses precious vestments and other religious textiles in the wonderfully carved cabinets; next to them are Baroque furniture, an altar and miniature family altar, brotherhood and miracle books, objects of sacred art. The founder Marquard von Schwendi can be seen here in a contemporary oil painting. After leaving the church, go through the door to the Pilgrims' Stairs and the present-day Capuchin monastery. The „Dekanstöckl", which Schwendi had built as a mini-palace, and the lovely St. Anne Fountain (Renaissance Pavilion from 1683) flank the exit onto the street. To the left, the street leads to the Austrian border 1 km away. To the right, though, there is a well-tended footpath leading down to Innstadt. Before descending the path, take in another magnificent view of the Inn with the Innbrücke and the opposite riverbank from above, stretching from the old town with the cathedral towers, the churches, and the town hall all the way over to the Veste Oberhaus proudly reigning over Passau. At the end of the promenade, walk a short distance along Fahrstraße before turning left at Jahnstraße. Just like the eastern extension of Römerstraße, this street follows along the old city wall which has been carefully restored in some places here, too. In 1988, the city renovated a particularly romantic spot in the southwest corner of the former city fortifications, the Bürgermeisterzwinger (Burgomaster's Outer Bailey). Its walls were built in 1408 under Prince Bishop von Hohenlohe, who also erected the two peel towers nearby. The imposing, round Peichterturm is an impressive indication of the well-fortified nature of the city on the Inn in the past. Opposite the bailey exit out to Jahnstraße, he strange, masoned column stumps in the middle of the lawn should catch your eye. They are part of the exterior grounds of the **Römermuseum (Roman Museum)** ❷⓿ which is located on the same site as the former Roman fort Boiotro. The original pillars, which consisted of several floors, used to rest on a deep foundation. Above ground, they were constructed of alternating tiers of bricks and tufa. There are maps on the observation terrace in the upper floor of the museum which can help visitors get an extensive overview of the site including reconstructed pillars and the foundation wall. Two other fragments of columns in the grounds outdoor are the remnants of milestones of the kind that once stood on the main roads of the Roman Empire long ago. The present museum building, a medieval domicile, was constructed upon a part of the foundation of the Roman fort. When builders began digging the foundation for a new kindergarten next to the building in 1974, a back-hoe operator

A view from the eastern vantage point at Mariahilf-Kloster over the Inn and the old town to Veste Oberhaus.

discovered the first remains of the wall, and the city decided to begin an extensive excavation effort. The museum was first opened on the basis of the finds made here in 1982 (with an addition in 1986) as a branch museum of the Pre-Historic State Collection in Munich. Start your tour of the museum in the upper floor with pre-history. There, you can see finds from the Stone Age (approx. 50,000 -1,800 BC) made in Upper Bavaria: earthenware for hunting and everyday life, weapons and jewellery made of copper, ceramic vessels, and some of the very first iron implements. During the Celtic Era (approx. 400 BC and later), the area around Passau was an important place of trade for graphite, which was extracted nearby and used in the manufacture of fireproof tableware. The collection of finds from Roman times is also extensive. The Romans built a total of three forts in Passau: the first ones were called „Batavis" (in the area of the old town) and „Boiadorum" (on the Inn approx. 800 m further upstream from the museum); the Romans then erected „Boiotro" to replace the two after they were destroyed by the Alemannians. As is obvious from the overview on the terrace, the foundation of the fort was laid out in the form of an irregular trapezoid; the foundation of at least two of its towers is fan-shaped. The glass cases mostly display weapons and utensils from that time period, some of the items even come from the Mediterranean area. The third

The Roman Museum of Fort Boiotro. In the foreground, the masonry column stumps from Roman times.

In the „Bürgermeisterzwinger", a part of the medieval city fortifications.

Boiotro Jupiter.

Roman bronze statuette of Victoria.

Roman gold coins (4th century).

Reverse side of the gold coin (see above).

room is dedicated to the Middle Ages. On display here are numerous burial furnishings, such as those from the grave of Archbishop Gregorius of Armenia, who was banished from his homeland, died in Passau in 1093, and found his final resting place in front of the high altar in the Church of Niedernburg Abbey.

The display cases in the ground floor also contain mainly exhibits from Roman times. Aside from numerous minor finds, two rather noteworthy bronze statuettes of the Roman goddess Victoria and Roman god Jupiter (both from around 200 AD) are on display there. Both statuettes were discovered during excavations in the area of the old town, as were finds from the late Classical Period such as coins, metal fittings, and jewellery. The two fragments of inscriptions on display in cases 23 and 24 are particularly significant: one comes from a military diploma (203 AD) like the ones retired soldiers received after 25 years of duty (conferring upon them, above all, the rights of Roman citizenship and the right to marry a non-Roman woman), and the other is part of a votive plaque (from around 240 AD). The basement is set up as a lapidarium, i.e. a collection of stone monuments. Most of them are tombstones or architectural fragments from Roman times.

Leaving the museum through the exit on the side facing the valley puts you on Ledergasse. The dark stones in the pavement are part of the north wall of the fort, which was also the location of the only entrance into the fort. Continuing along the narrow street to the left a few meters, you come to one of the former four city gates of the city on the Inn. It and its bastion were erected in 1412 soon after completion of the city wall. The gate was named Severintor (formerly Peichertor) after the church nearby. The wooden pulleys on the exterior, at one time used to hold the drawbridge rope, are still intact. The passage through the gate leads straight up to **Severinskirche (The Church of Saint Severinus) ㉑** in the

The Roman Museum of Fort Boiotro:
Open: March to middle November (closed in winter), Tu. to Su. 10 AM- 4 PM. Phone: 0851/34769.
Museum tours: *on the 1st and 3rd Wednesday of each month from 5-6 PM. For reservations, phone: 0851/34769.*

Severinskirche: Outer wall with old tombstones.

middle of the main cemetery of Passau. Just like the city gate nearby, the apparently towerless church is named after St. Severinus, who came to the region on the Danube and Inn as a missionary around 460. He built a small monastery for a few monks and a singlenave basilica, the foundation of which was discovered underneath the floor of the present church in 1976. Around the turn of the millennium, a new structure was erected (partially based on the wall of the early Christian church) with a transept on the west side, where present-day visitors can see the annex containing the „Severinszelle" („Severinus's Cell"). During the Roma-

Severinskirche: late Baroque wooden figure: Christ at rest.

nesque period, the nave was extended to its present length. The late Gothic choir and the low tower were added in 1476. Until 1968, St. Severinus was a parish church; today, it is a cemetery church of the St. Severinus Parish, which now has St. Gertraud as its parish church. The modern crucifix made of limestone dominates the interior of Severinskirche. It and the altar are both creations of Leopold Hafner, although the altar contains numerous relics from early Christian times. The tabernacle composed of red marble and made in 1600 in Renaissance style is a rarity. The Roman tombstone, used today as a font for holy water, is even older. The inscription it bears tells of „the household gods of the Illyrian tax collector Faustinian", thereby testifying to its pre-Christian origins. In contrast, the knocker on the door to the sacristy and two statues of saints in the choir come from late Gothic times (around 1500). The high relief „The Passing of the Virgin Mary" located in the „Severinszelle" and some of the tombstones (from 1348 and later), such as the heavily embellished epitaph of a widow named Sturm, are about the same age. The most noteworthy works from Baroque times are the three large paintings with the images of saints and the carved statue of „Christ at Rest". There are numerous, valuable tombstones on the outer wall of the church also dating back to Gothic times. Leaving the old cemetery around St. Severinus, the

View of the old town and St. Stephen's Cathedral from Fünferlsteg.

Innsteg, which natives affectionately refer to as Fünferlsteg, takes you back over the river. On the way, you can enjoy the beautiful view of the two parts of the city. If you turn to the left at Innstraße, directly behind the promenade, you come to St. Nikolai Church, which has an 11th century crypt. Today, the church is part of the **modern university ㉒** (9000 students), which carries on the tradition of the prince bishopric city as a centre of education and culture. It is more than a coincidence that the Augustinian monastery was once located here. Aside from their pastoral

duties, the Augustinian monks were also devoted to scholarly edification. Consequently, a line can be traced from the monasteries down to the cathedral school of the legendary Bishop Pilgrim, the preparatory school and university of the Jesuits, the Prince Bishops' Academy, the four preparatory schools still existing today, and the Philosophic Theological University (the direct predecessor of the University of Passau). Augustinerstraße, named after the monastery, runs into the „Kleiner Exerzierplatz", site of major festivals for the residents of Passau

The „Innpromenade" is on the riverbank to the left.

University of Passau.

to this day: the city has celebrated the „Herbstdult" (an autumn festival) for 800 years. The „Maidult" in the spring was added some time later. Both of these public festivals were originally trade fairs and now attract visitors from all over. For some time now, they have been taking place at Kohlbruck Exhibition Park. The parade ground (Exerzierplatz) and the site of the Nibelungenhalle are to be redesigned to create a "New Centre". The centre of traffic in Passau, Ludwigsplatz, is just behind it. Ludwigsstraße leads away from the square in the direction of the cathedral and compensates for the inconvenience of modern traffic by bringing pedestrians to the pedestrian precinct. On the main axis of Passau's pedestrian precinct, you can stroll along and have a look at any of the numerous shops or take a break at one of the many cafés and restaurants. To get back to the cathedral, take Grabengasse and Carlonengasse, both closed to automobile traffic.

The
"New middle".

Neue Mitte. New
Shopping Center

The Hals District

A drive along the east bank of the Ilz by car brings visitors to the present-day Hals district in just a few minutes. However, if you're not in a hurry, we recommend taking a walk along the west bank of the river. Along the way, pedestrians have a nice view of the former market square at the foot of the castle ruins from above. The location became quite popular around 1900 on account of the moor water from the Ilz, used to operate a spa. Its famous guests from four continents included Peter Rosegger and the composer Franz Lehar, who wrote his first operetta in Bad Hals. Old inns on the market square to either side of the Rathaus (the town hall from 1510) bear witness to this era. The pillory standing in front of the Rathaus is a symbol of medieval justice. Up on the hill, the castle of the „Nobility of Hals" once ruled over the settlement and the traffic entering and leaving the valley. Its owners guarded the profitable rafting traffic from the Bavarian Forest and especially the pearl fishery in the Ilz. Its soft water was particularly conducive to raising and keeping river pearl clams, which, for their part, produced particularly large, highquality

pearls. This turned pearl fishing into a good source of income starting back in the 15th century, and pearls came into vogue for both the ruling class and peasants alike, who secretly schemed to secure a portion of the harvest. Overexploitation, logging, and, in recent times, changes in the environmental conditions have taken a great toll on the number of clams to this day. It is only the efforts of animal protectionists that have saved them from complete extinction. For nature lovers, we recommend hiking upstream along the Ilz from the castle (about 3 hours). In the former log chute, you can still see the bridge-shaped logchute barrier and log-driving tunnel, telltale signs of the logging. Aside from that, there are also rare species of plants and animals (the kingfisher, the aquatic blackbird) on one of the last unspoiled natural riverbanks in Germany. Along the way, attractive inns and the refreshing water of the artificial lake invite hikers to rest a while. Hikers can cross the Ilz over the concrete dam and return on the other bank or can take another one of the trails in the well marked trail system.

The Hals District in Passau on both sides of the Ilz is known as one of the most beautiful spots in the region. The ruins of the medieval castle clearly stand out against the wooded hills of the surroundings above the former spa town.

A winter fairy tale

Outings in the Vicinity

Cycling tours:
Eight long-distance cycling paths lead from Passau along the Danube and Inn rivers.

Tour Austrian Biketrail:
down the Danube to Vienna by way of Linz and Wachau.

Tour de Baroque:
up the Danube past Regensburg, then through the Altmühltal and Sulztal valleys to Neumarkt/Oberpfalz.

Isar cycling trail:
up the Danube until just before Deggendorf, then along the Isar to Munich by way of Plattling-Landshut-Freising.

Vilstal cycling trail:
up the Danube to Vilshofen, then on through the Vilstal to Vilsburg (near Landshut).

„German Danube" cycling trail: up the Danube to its source in Donaueschingen. Rottal cycling trail: along the Inn to Neustadt/Inn, then along the Rott to Eggenfelden by way of Pfarrkirchen.

Tauern cycling trail:
through the Inn Valley past Braunau, then through the Salzachtal, by way of Salzburg, to Krimml at the foot of the Hohen Tauern.

Inn cycling trail:
along the Inn, by way of Wasserburg/Inn - Rosenheim - Kufstein - Innsbruck - Landeck and St. Moritz, to Maloja (Oberengadin/Switzerland, at the foot of the Bernina Mountain Range).

Tourist-Information Passauer Land
www. passauer-land.de
Tel. 0851/397-600

Riverboat trips:

(also see the advertisement on p. 8)
The Danube riverboat line Wurm & Köck offers a variety of opportunities to experience one of Europe's loveliest river valleys by boat. The experience is heightened by the elegant furnishings and fine cuisine onboard, as well as the rich cultural landscape on the section of the river between Deggendorf and Linz. Please note that an ID-card is required on all cross-border trips; you can also shop duty-free onboard.

Asbach: (35 km)
Ehemaliges Benediktinerkloster Asbach (5 km Richtung Griesbach). Eine Zweigstelle des Bayerischen Nationalmuseums.

Tittling (20 km toward Grafenau):
Bavarian Forest Historical Village, expansive openair museum operated by the hoteliers Mr. and Mrs. Höltl (see glass museum).

Hot springs resorts:
Bad Füssing, Tel. 08531/975580
Bad Griesbach, Tel. 08532/79240

Eging am See: (20 km)
Westerncity Pullman

By car:

Hindling: (8km)
A vantage point offering one of the prettiest views of Passau. To get there, drive to the Achleiten border checkpoint, then turn left immediately.

Obernzell on the Danube: (20 km)
Palace museum with an interesting collection of crockery, some of it made of graphite, picture gallery. To get there, follow the road on the left bank of the Danube.

Aldersbach: (30 km)
baroque rococo convent.

Altenmarkt/Osterhofen: (25 km)
baroque Asambasilika.

Hauzenberg „Steinwelten":
Granite centre in Bavaria Forest.

Tips and addresses from A to Z

Telephone area code for Passau: 0851 +49 851/
Postal code D – 94032

Information:
Tourist information: at Rathausplatz 2, 94032 Passau, phone 95598-0, FAX 95598-30 or 95598-31, Easter-Sept. Mo.-Fr. 8.30 AM-6 PM, Sat., Su., and holidays 9 AM-4 PM; Oct.-Easter, Mo.-Thur. 8.30 AM-5 PM, Fr. 8.30 AM-4 PM, Sat., Su. 10 AM-3PM.
Bahnhofstrasse 28, 94032 Passau, Eastern-Sep.: Mon.-Fri. 9 AM-12 PM + 12.30 AM-5 PM, Sat., Su., holidays 10.30 AM-3.30 PM, Oct.-Eastern: Mon.-Thur. 9 AM-12 PM + 12.30 PM-5 PM, Fri. 9 AM-12 PM + 12.30 PM-4 PM, Sa. 10.30 AM-3.30 PM.
E-Mail:tourist-info@passau.de, www.passau.de

Emergency telephone numbers:
Fire: 112; police: 110; emergency medical services: 19222

Bicycle repairs and shop:
Denk bike+outdoor Ludwigstraße 22, phone 31450
RENT A BIKE, BIKEAMBULANZ©, Bahnhofstraße 29, Hbf./Westgebäude, Tel. 0851/9662570 oder 0151/12834224
Fahrradladen, Wittgasse 9, Tel. 72226;
Fahrrad-Klinik, Bräugasse 10, phone 33411

Camping:
Passau-Irring, phone 08546/633; tent campgrounds on the Ilz, phone 41457

Car hire service: (among others)
Europcar, Bahnhofstrasse 29, phone 54235, Sixt, phone 959690

Cinemas:
Cineplex Nibelungenpl. 5a, phone 9883550
Metropolis, phone 752815;
Scharfrichterkino, phone 2655

Emergency road service by ADAC
(National German Automobile Club):
24 hrs.-a-day, phone 0180/2222222

German Rail (Deutsche Bahn AG):

Passau Central Station (Hauptbahnhof), information 01805-996633

Hospitals:
Passau Hospital, phone 5300-0;
Private Hospital Dr. Hellge, phone 7008-0;
Children's Hospital, phone 72050

Lost-property office:
At town hall, Schrottgasse, phone 396-225 or 295

Museums:
see notes on pp. 19, 33, 53, 60

Parking (in the Old Town):
see city map

Police:
Niebelungenstraße 17, phone 95110

Main-Post office:
Bahnhofstraße 27, phone 95950, Mon.-Fri. 8 AM-6 PM, Sat. 8 AM-12 PM.

Riverboat trips:
Danube riverboat line Wurm + Köck, Höllgasse 26, phone 929292, FAX 35518; also see the note on p. 8+87.

Shuttle bus:
April-Oct. between Veste Oberhaus and Rathausplatz, Mo-Fr 10 AM-5 PM every half-hour Sa, Sun & Holidays 10 AM-6 PM every half-hour

Sight-seeing tours:
Eckerl-Reisen, phone 0851/34262

swimming baths:
Passauer Erlebnisbad peb open throughout the year with indoor, outdoor and "Balineum" wellness swimming pools

Theatre:
Theatre im fürstbischöflichen Opernhaus, phone 9291910; Theatre im Scharfrichterhaus, phone 35900

Youth hostel: phone 49378-0

Notes

View from the Austrian town of Hinding: An evening mood over the

„floating city" between the Danube and Inn.

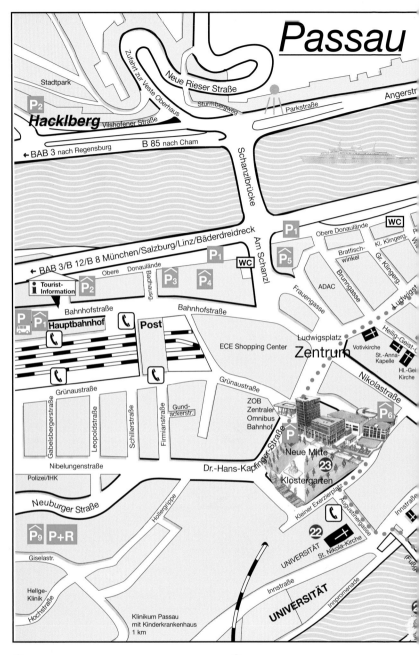

Passau

1. Tourist-Information, Altes Rathaus
2. Rathaus (ab 1393, mit prächtigen Sälen)
3. Museum Moderner Kunst
4. Dreiflüsse-Eck (Ortspitze)
5. Waisenhaus
6. Kloster Niedernburg (Gisela Grab)
7. Residenzplatz
8. Neue Residenz
9. Domschatz- und Diözesanmuseum
10. St.-Stephans-Dom (größte Domorgel der Welt)
11. Pfarrkirche St. Paul
12. Höllgasse
13. Glasmuseum
14. Veste Oberhaus
15. Salvatorkirche